'The Coathanger' (Sydney Harbour Bridge)

Foreword

Quite obviously, migrants and visitors to Australia must have difficulty in understanding many words or expressions used by Australians in their everyday speech. This pocket book is an easy reference to help visitors or recent migrants understand much of the seemingly inexplicable slang they will hear from day to day

I should like to dedicate this book to my Aunty Dot and her faithful dog 'Bluey'.

P.H.

acid - put the **acid** on - (ask for money or a favour)

Akubra (brand name used for a hat)

alec - smart **alec** - (a showoff)

alkie (person who drinks too much alcohol)

Anzac (soldier who fought at Gallipoli)

apples - **she's apples** - (everything is in order)

arvo (afternoon)

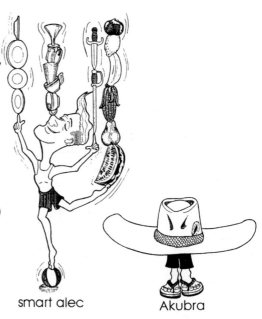

smart alec

Akubra

Auntie (The Australian Broadcasting Commission)

Australian salute (hand going up to brush a fly away)

backblocks (land far from towns)

bagman (handles illicit money)

bail up (hold up at gunpoint)

Bananabender (someone from Queensland)

bangers (sausages)

Australian salute

Bananabender

barbie (barbecue)

barney (an argument or fight)

bash - have a **bash** - (to try something)

bathers (swimming costume)

battler (hard-working person)

Bay - the **Bay** - (Long Bay Jail)

beaut (a word that describes anything favourable) - a **beaut** car

barbie

barney

beauty - 'you beauty' - (expressing happiness)

beer-gut (a large stomach from drinking beer)

belt up ('be quiet' or 'shut up')

berley (scatter bait on water to attract fish)

bib - to stick one's **bib** in - (to interfere)

Bible-basher (anyone who is religious)

big-note - to **bignote** oneself - (to make out you are better than you are)

belt up

beer gut

billy (can for boiling water over a fire
to make tea)

bindi-eye (a weed in lawns that has
prickles)

binge (drinking party)

bite - put the **bite** on someone - (ask
for a loan of money, or a favour)

bitser (anything made of bits and pieces,
a mongrel dog)

black stump - this side of the **black stump** -
(imaginary landmark where
civilisation ends)

blind Freddie - even **blind Freddie** could
see that - (an imaginary
blind person)

bitser

billy

Blake - a Joe **Blake** - (a snake)

block - do or lose one's block (lose one's temper or take leave of one's senses)

blow (to brag or boast)

blow - to strike a **blow -** (to start work)

blowhard (person who talks or brags a great deal)

blowie (blowfly)

blow-in (someone who comes to the house unexpectedly)

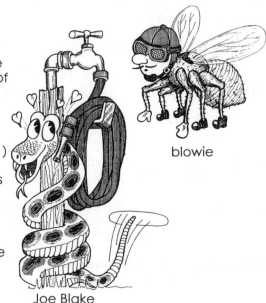

blowie

Joe Blake

blow through (go away)

bludge (live off someone else)

bludger (a person who lives off someone else, or doesn't pay his or her way)

blue (a quarrel or brawl)

blue rinse set (wealthy old ladies from Sydney or Melbourne)

bluey (a type of cattle dog)

Bobby Dazzler - She is a **Bobby Dazzler** at dancing - (someone who is an expert)

blue rinse set

bodgie (not well made or done) -
    bodgie job

bog - **Bog** in, don't wait - (eat up the
    meal)

bomb (an old car or a second-hand
    car in need of repair)

bombed out (drunk, or high on drugs)

Bondi Tram - He shot through like a
    Bondi Tram - (moved
    quickly)

bone - to point the **bone** - (Aboriginal
    curse
    that causes a person to die or
    come to some harm)

bonkers (crazy or mad)

bomb

bombed out

bonzer (excellent) - a **bonzer** person

boomer (large kangaroo or anything very large)

booze bus (bus used by police for random breath testing)

bottler (good or excellent)

bower bird (person who collects seemingly worthless objects)

box seat (the best position)

breakers (surfing waves)

box seat

Buckley's - to have **Buckley's** chance of winning - (no chance at all)

brumby (wild horse)

bull (nonsense) 'Don't talk **bull**.'

Bullamakanka (imaginary backward place far from the city)

bulldust (talk that is nonsense or lies)

bullet - to be given the **bullet** - (sacked)

bull's wool (an unlikely story)

get the bullet

brumby

bumper - not worth a **bumper** - (useless - a 'bumper' being a cigarette butt)

bundle - to drop one's **bundle** - (give up or lose one's nerve)

bundy (clock which records time on a worker's card as he or she enters or leaves work)

bung it on (pretend you are better than you are)

bunny (victim or person weak at sport)

bunyip (monster in Aboriginal legend that lived in water-holes and devoured people)

burl - give it a **burl** - (try something)

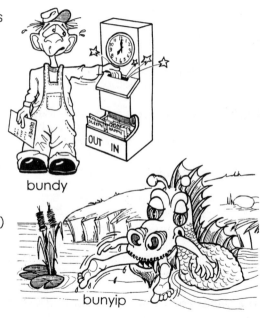

bundy

bunyip

bush (country area in Australia)

bushed (lost)

bush carpenter (rough and ready tradesperson)

bush lawyer (person who professes to know about the law but has had no legal training)

bushman's clock (kookaburra - bird that laughs at sunrise and sunset)

bushranger (term used for a thief - from the early days in Australia when bushrangers roamed the country on horseback)

bushwhacker (uncouth country person)

bushman's clock

bushwhacker

BYO (bring your own liquor to a party or restaurant)

carpeted (brought before someone to explain wrong-doing)

cashed up (having plenty of money)

chain - drag the **chain** - (lag behind)

chalkie (schoolteacher)

chiak (taunt or tease)

chips - to be spitting **chips** - (be very angry)

BYO

chook (hen, or sometimes a term for woman)

choom (Englishman)

chop - get in for one's **chop** - (obtain one's share)

choppers (teeth or helicopters)

chuck - to **chuck** in - (contribute money)

chuck - (vomit) - to chuck up

chunder (vomit) - to **chunder**

choppers

chook

clobber (clothing, or to strike someone)

clued up (knowing much about a subject)

cluey (having much knowledge)

coathanger (The Sydney Harbour Bridge)

cobber (friend)

cockatoo (person keeping a lookout when a crime is committed)

cocky (farmer)

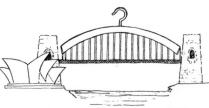

Coathanger

cocky

cocky's friend (fencing wire - used to repair things)

cocky's delight (golden syrup)

cooee (within easy reach) She lives within **coee,**

cop shop (police station)

coot - **coot** of a job - (difficult job)

coot (person - usually a difficult one)

cossie (bathing costume)

cossie

coot

cot case (someone who is ill in bed)

cove (person)

cow - having a **cow** of a time -
(having an unhappy time)

crack hardy (pretend to be happy
or well)

crack it (succeed in doing
something)

cracker - not worth a **cracker** -
(worthless)

crawl (be nice to someone in authority
to gain favour)

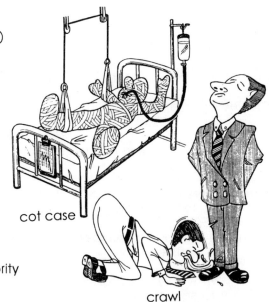

cot case

crawl

crook (broken down, no good or sick)

crook - go **crook** on - (scold)

Croweater (person from South Australia)

crows - stone the **crows !** - (expression of surprise)

cruel - **cruel** someone's pitch (ruin or spoil their chances)

crumpet - not worth a **crumpet** - (worthless)

crust - What do you do for a **crust** ? (to earn money)

stone the crows

crook

Cup - the Melbourne **Cup** - (annual horse race)

cuppa (cup of tea or coffee)

cut - (angry)- He is **cut** about it.

dag (person who is dull or not much fun)

damper (early form of bread, flour and water cooked in hot ashes)

dekko (look)- Have a **dekko!**

deli (delicatessen shop)

damper

dag

demons (police, generally in plain clothes)

dero (derelict or destitute person)

dice (throw away)

digger (gold miner or Australian soldier)

dill (stupid person)

dilly (stupid or foolish)

dingbats (mad)

dingbats

dero

dingo (sneaky person)

dinky die (truthful)

dinkum - fair **dinkum** - (genuine, true)

dinkum oil (true inside information)

dinner - done like a **dinner** - (well and truly beaten)

dip ones lid (raise one's hat)

dip out (lose or miss out)

dingo

dirty - do the **dirty** - (use unfair tactics)

dish up - to **dish up** - (to beat at sport)

divvy (share the proceeds)

do over (beat up)

dob in (inform or tell tales about someone)

dog's disease (influenza)

dog's breakfast (untidy presentation of something)

dog's breakfast

dole bludger (someone drawing
unemployment benefits
when work is available)

dong (hit or punch someone)

donga (gully or simple shelter)

donkey vote (vote by numbering
candidates in order they
appear on a ballot
paper)

double drummer (kind of cicada)

down - having a **down** on someone -
(holding a grudge)

Down Under (Australia)

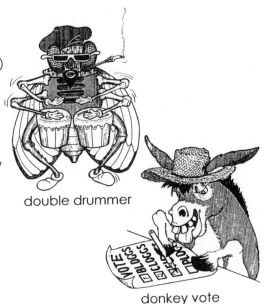

double drummer

donkey vote

drack (ugly)

drop (when a wicket falls in a cricket match)

drum (sound advice or information)

duff (steal cattle)

dumper (large wave that pushes surfer into the sand)

dunny (outside toilet)

earbash (talk a great deal)

drack

dumper

esky (portable ice box for drinks or food)

euchered - (tired out)

Eyetie (Italian)

fangs - put the **fangs** into someone -
(borrow money or ask a favour)

farm - buying back the **farm** - (buying
back anything Australian from
overseas investors)

fat cats (highly paid public servants)

fence - over the **fence** - (not reasonable)

esky

fat cats

fly - give it a **fly** - (try)

fossick (search for gold or precious stones)

full (drunk)

furphy (idle rumour)

Gabba - Woollangabba - (Queensland's cricket ground)

galah (fool)

galoot (stupid and clumsy-looking person)

galoot

gander (look) - Take a **gander** at him!

gap (cliff in Sydney where people commit suicide)

garbo (garbage collector)

gargle (a drink) I am off for a gargle !

gibber (boulder or large stone)

give away (stop doing something)

goer (a racehorse or person that tries hard)

goer

good nick (in good condition or health)

good-oh (expression used when agreeing to something)

good on you (well done)

graft (work)

grafter (hard worker)

Granny (Sydney Morning Herald newspaper)

Granny Smith (a variety of apple first grown in Sydney)

grafter

in good nick

greenie (conservationist who supports bans on demolishing old buildings or excess tree felling)

grey nurse (type of shark)

grog (any alcoholic drink)

grotty (dirty)

grouse (excellent)

guernsey - get a **guernsey** - (be chosen for a sporting team)

gully (small valley)

greenie

gutser - to come a **gutser** - (have a fall)

hammer - to be on someone's **hammer** (put pressure on someone)

head - pull your **head** in - (be quiet or shut up)

hens' teeth - as scarce as **hens' teeth** - (non existent)

herbs - give it the **herbs** - (accelerate or give it more power)

home - **home** and hosed - (finished with time to spare)

homestead (main house on a farm)

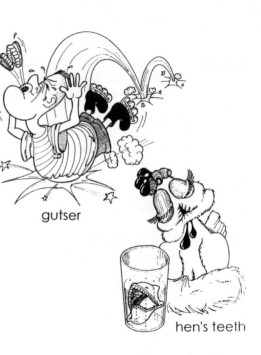

gutser

hen's teeth

hooks - put the **hooks** into someone - (ask for a loan or favour)

hooray (cheerio or goodbye)

hoot (money) - It is worth a heap of **hoot**.

hostie (air hostess)

hump (carry) - We had to hump our bags.

humpy (Aboriginal bark hut)

hunt (chase away) - **Hunt** that fly away!

hostie

humpy

in it - be **in it** - (appeal to join an activity)

in the bag (as good as done)

jack - to be **jack** of something - (fed up)

jack up (refuse to do something)

jackaroo (young male working on a farm to gain experience)

jackass - the laughing **jackass** - (kookaburra, a bird that laughs)

Jake - She's **Jake** mate - (Everything is all right my friend)

laughing jackass

jack up

Jessie - more hide than **Jessie** -
(cheeky, Jessie was a zoo elephant)

jillaroo (young female working on a
farm to gain experience)

Joe Blow (the average man in the
street)

joey (baby kangaroo)

John (policeman)

joker (chap or fellow) - He is a pleasant
joker.

journo (journalist)

joey

jillaroo

jumbuck (sheep)

kick the bucket (die)

kick the tin (put in money for a collection)

Kiwi (new Zealander)

knocker - cash on the **knocker** - (immediate payment)

knuckle sandwich (punch in the mouth)

Kybosh - put the Kybosh on it - (put a stop to something)

knuckle sandwich

kick the bucket

lair (a person who shows off)

larriken (young noisy person who is apt to get into mischief)

Larry - as happy as **Larry** - (very happy)

lash - have a **lash** - (try doing something)

lay-by (put a deposit on an item in a shop, then pay the balance later)

legal eagle (lawyer)

light on (short in weight or numbers)

lair

legal eagle

lizards - starve the **lizards** -
(exclamation of disbelief)

load - get a **load** of that - (have a
look at that)

lob - to **lob** in - (arrive)

lolly (sweet - English , candy- American)

lolly - do one's **lolly** - (lose one's temper)

lollywater (soft drink)

loo (lavatory)

loo

DO NOT FEED

starve the lizards

lousy (mean with money)

lucky - Strike me **lucky** ! -
(exclamation of surprise)

lurk - a good **lurk** to make money-
(a good scheme)

Maroons (Queensland Rugby League
team)

meat axe - as mad as a **meat axe** -
(crazy)

merchant (usually an undesirable
person - con -**merchant**,
standover **merchant**)

metho (methylated spirits)

as mad as a meat axe

Mick (Roman Catholic)

middy (measure of beer in a glass)

milko (milkman)

mockers - put the **mockers** on someone -
(cast a spell on someone or
give them bad luck)

moonlight flit (leave at night without
paying the rent)

mossie (mosquito)

motser (a large win when gambling)

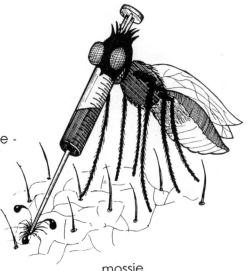

mossie

mulga (acacia tree, but also used to describe any desolate region)

mullet - be like a stunned **mullet** - (be in a dazed condition)

narked (angry) - He is **narked** by your remarks.

necessary (money) Have you the **necessary** ?

Ned Kelly (name of a famous Australian bushranger given to anyone dishonest)

neddy (a horse)

neg driving (short for 'negligent driving', a traffic offence)

Ned Kelly

Never - Never (areas of Australia far from towns and cities)

nick off (move away quickly)

nips - put the **nips** in - (borrow money)

nit - to keep **nit** - (keep watch - usually when a crime is being committed)

no-hoper (useless person)

nong (stupid person)

put the nips in

nong

nose - on the **nose** - (smelly)

nuddy - in the **nuddy** - (in the nude)

nuggety (stocky or thickset)

ocker (uncouth Australian who speaks with a broad Australian accent)

off sider (friend)- Meet my **off-sider** from work.

oil (information) Give me the good **oil.**

old country (country of origin - was mainly U.K.)

nuggety

in the nuddy

oldie (term used for older people)

onkus (something mechanical that is not working)

oodles (plenty) - She has **oodles** of money.

outback (country far away from cities)

out of the box (special or outstanding)

out to grass (retired)

Oz (Australia)

onkus

oldie

pack - gone to the **pack** - (run down or deteriorated)

packing them (scared)

Paddo (Paddington - suburb of Sydney)

paddock (fenced area of farm land)

pakapoo ticket - like a **pakapoo** ticket - (not orderly, untidy)

pan out (turn out or happen)

perk (special privilege)

packing them

gone to the pack

pigs (police)

pimp (sneaky person who reports
things to the boss)

pineapple - get the rough end of the
pineapple - (be treated
unfairly)

Pitt Street - **Pitt Street** farmer - (business
or professional man who
owns a farm)

plonk (cheap wine)

poddy (a calf)

pokies (poker machines)

rough end of
the pineapple

Pitt Street farmer

pollies (politicians)

Pom, Pommy (English person)

pong (smell) - That fertilizer **pongs**.

possie (position , place to sit or stand)

poppy - a tall poppy - (someone earning a lot of money or in a high position)

port (a case for carrying personal things)

prawn - come the raw **prawn** - (expression used when people feel they are being fooled)

pong

prezzie (present or gift)- a birthday **prezzie**

pull up stakes (leave somewhere)

putty - up to **putty** - (useless)

race - not in the **race** (no chance at all)

rack off (get lost or go away)

Rafferty's Rules (no rules at all)

ratbag (stupid or odd person)

pull up stakes

rathouse (lunatic asylum)

ratty (odd or peculiar)

Red Ned (cheap wine)

rego (motor vehicle registration fee)

rip - wouldn't it **rip** you - (expression of annoyance)

ripper (used to describe something excellent)

rockhopper (person who fishes from rocks)

wouldn't it rip you

rockhopper

rocking-horse manure (expression to describe something that doesn't exist)

ropeable (very angry, needs tying down)

rort (a dishonest scheme)

rouse on (shout at someone angrily)

rubbedy (hotel, rubbedy dub rhymes with pub)

rustbucket (car or ship that is very rusty)

saddle up (get ready for work)

rocking-horse manure·

sandgroper (person born in Western Australia)

school (group of drinkers or gamblers)

schoolie (schoolteacher)

schooner (large glass of beer)

screamer - a two pot **screamer** - (someonewho easily becomes drunk)

scrub (anywhere far from towns)

serve - give someone a **serve** - (tell someone off)

schooner

serve

shag - like a **shag** on a rock - (all alone
    - a shag is a sea bird)

sharkbait (person who swims beyond other
        swimmers in the surf)

sheila (a girl or woman)

sherbet (beer) - 'He's fond of the
        sherbet -

shoot through (go off somewhere)

shout (buy drinks for others)

shrewdie (cunning person)

shag on a rock

sickie (a day off work - taken if sick or not)

silent cop (round yellow metal marker on a road to prevent drivers cutting corners)

silvertail (wealthy person)

skerrick (a small piece)

skillion (a lean-to with sloping roof attached to a building)

skite (to boast)

slather - having open **slather** - (free to do anything one wants)

silvertail

silent cop

sling - to **sling** off at - (to be rude or criticise someone)

slug (charge too much for something)

smackers (dollars)

Smithy (Sir Charles Kingsford-Smith , Australian pioneer aviator)

smoko (short break from work to smoke, eat or drink)

smoodge (be affectionate or ask lovingly)

snack (something done easily

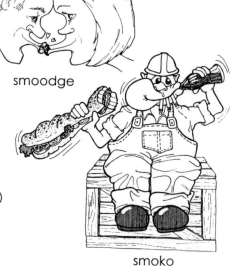

smoodge

smoko

snags (sausages)

snakey (bad-tempered or not in a
       good mood)

snowdropping (stealing clothing from
       washing lines or hoists)

Socceroos (Australian Soccer team)

sook (timid person or cry-baby)

sort (girl or woman)

southerly buster (cool gusty wind that
       springs up at the end of a
       day in summer)

snowdropping

sook

spiel (dishonest talk by a salesperson)

spieler (dishonest person who uses
    trickery)

spin - a rough **sp**in - (a rough time)

spine basher (a person who sleeps a
    great deal)

spit chips (be very angry) She's **spitting chips.**

sport - How are you **sport** ? (general
    term used in opening
    conversation)

spring chicken - no **spring chicken** -
    (no longer young)

spine basher

a rough spin

spruik (talk like a circus announcer)

squattocracy (name given to old farming families who are likened to aristocrats)

squiz (take a quick inquisitive look)

steamed up (be angry)

sticky-beak (inquisitive person)

stiff (out of luck) He had **stiff** luck.

stonkered (very tired or drunk)

steamed up

squiz

stoush (a fight)

strides (men's long trousers)

stubby (small bottle of beer)

surfie (person who spends much time
at the beach surfing or board
riding)

swagman (person who travelled
carrying all his possessions)

sweat - no **sweat** - (no problem -
everything will be fine)

sweat on (waiting for something to
happen)

swagman

surfie

sweet - she'll be **sweet** - (everything will be all right)

swifty - pull a **swifty** - (deceive someone by trickery)

tarp ((tarpaulin)

Tassie (Tasmania)

tee up (make an arrangement)'
I'll **tee up** a meeting.'

tinny (lucky, or a can of beer)

togs (swimming costume)

tinny

swifty

trannie (portable radio)

trot - a bad **trot** - (bad series of happenings)

trumps (a likeable person)

trunks (male swimming shorts)

truckie (truck driver)

tucker (food)

turps (liquor)

truckie

trannie

uey - do a **uey** - (make a U-turn when driving a car)

uni (university)

ute (utility truck that carries goods)

wake up - to **wake up** to something - (to know exactly what is going on)

Wallabies (Australian Rugby Union team)

washer (flannel used to wash one's face)

watering-hole (pub or bar used by a regular group)

Wallabies

uey

weekender (cottage where a family can spend the week-end - usually by the sea)

well in (doing well or liked by somebody)

whack (a ration or share of something)

whacked (very tired)

whacko (expression of joy or approval)

wharfie (dock worker)

whinge (complain)

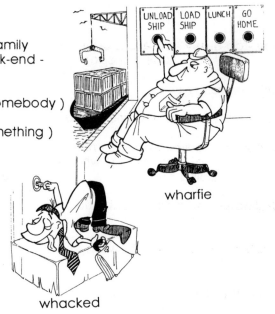

wharfie

whacked

whinger (one who complains)

whip - fair crack of the **whip** - (an expression meaning to act fairly)

willy willy (a dusty wind that spirals upwards)

Windies (West Indies cricket team)

Woop Woop (imaginary place far from towns and cities)

works (everything) - 'I'll have the works on the menu.'

word - **word** him up - (tell him)

willy willy

worries - no **worries** - (there are no problems)

wouldn't it (abbreviation for wouldn't it make you angry, sick etc)

wowser (person who does not drink and has no other vices)

yabbie (freshwater crayfish found in dams or creeks)

yack or **yacker** (talk) 'She is always **yacking.**'

yakker (work) 'He hates hard **yakker.**'

you beaut (expression of joy or approval)

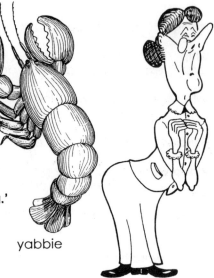

yabbie

wowser